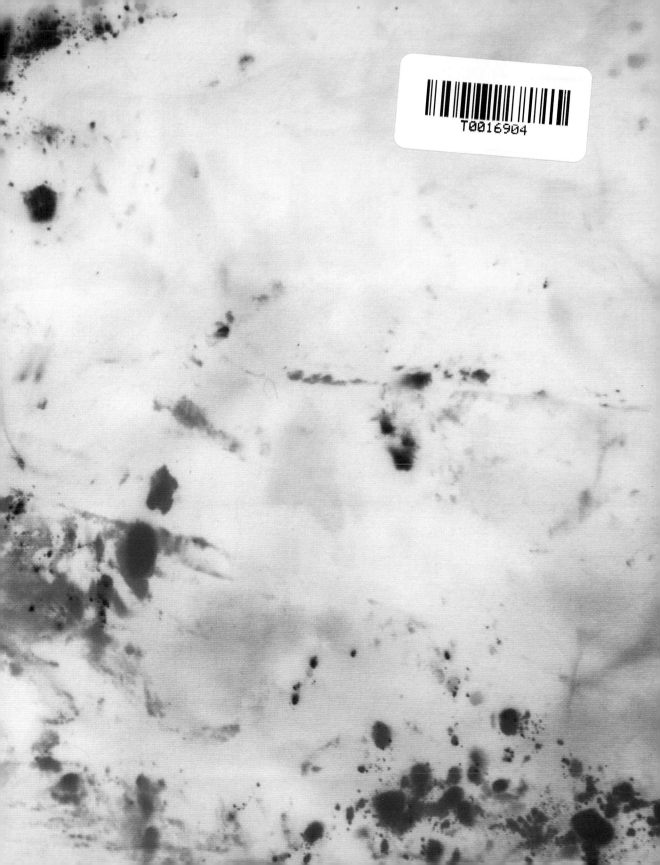

Tie
Dye

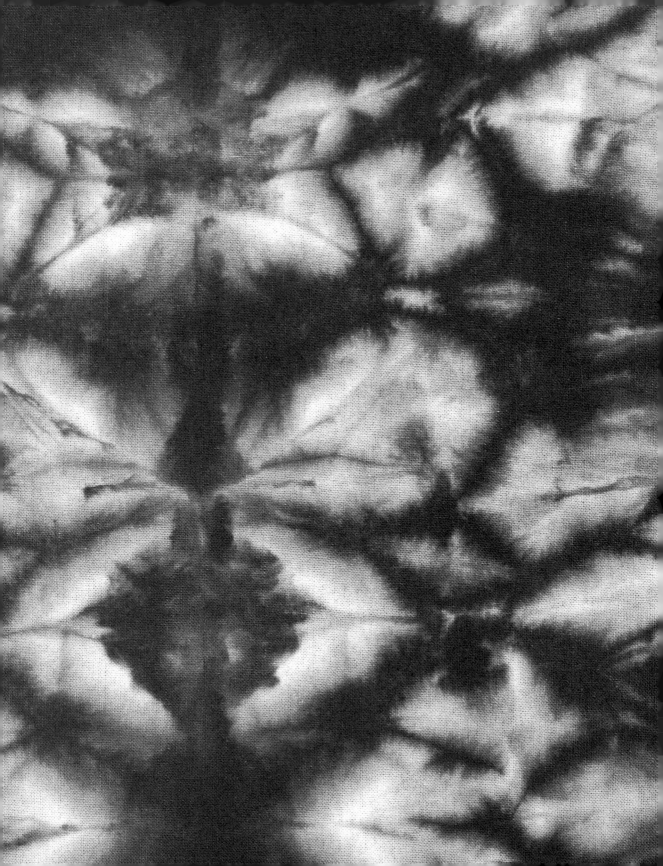

Tie
Dye

Fashion from Hippie to Chic

Kate McNamara
with an essay by Molly Young

RIZZOLI
NEW YORK

New York · Paris · London · Milan

First published in the United States of America in 2022
by Rizzoli International Publications, Inc.
300 Park Avenue South
New York, NY 10010
Rizzoliusa.com

Distributed in the U.S. trade by Random House, New York

Art © artists and photographers
Text © Kate McNamara, Molly Young
Front cover: Photographed and styled by Sarah Louise
Stedeford and Santi Rodriguez for ASAI.

Editor: Julie Schumacher
In-House Design Coordinator: Olivia Russin
Photography Manager: Supriya Malik
Photography Assistant: Owen Madigan
Production Manager: Barbara Sadick
Publisher: Charles Miers

ISBN-13: 978-0-8478-6534-5
Library of Congress Catalog Control Number: 2021948771

2022 2023 2024 2025 2026 / 10 9 8 7 6 5 4 3 2 1

Printed in China

Contents

Tie-dye:
The Social Network
by Kate McNamara

Tie-dye as a motif, textile, and art form bridges cultural phenomena. It is a visual icon that persists and continues to be resurrected wash after cultural wash. A symbol of protest, self-expression, and independence, tie-dye has a foothold in high fashion and music. It has become the flag in which to plant one's lifestyle. While tie-dye is a centuries-old technique used around the world, in the United States, it has become an umbrella term, coined to address a wide range of dye techniques originally made mainstream during the "free-love" sixties.

While the country was mired in politics of conformity and a gratuitous war, the demands for individual expression, fanciful experiences, and communal participation were vital to a utopic reimagining of oneself. A generation of young Americans sought to embrace what they had been expected to suppress: equality, gender, sexuality, spirituality, anti-war sentiments, and individuality. Tie-dye signified an experience and a visual form of individualism. Tie-dye was, to paraphrase the novelist Ken Kesey, one of many tickets to being "on the bus." Music captained this rebellious trip as artists, taking cues from the improvisational methods of blues and jazz, created cosmic harmonies that tie-dye visually represented so well. From The Rolling Stones to Janis Joplin, the Grateful Dead to Jimi Hendrix, and from the thousands of attendees at Woodstock to the stage of Fillmore West, tie-dye clearly signified something bigger than psychedelia—it was a motif emblematic of a youth movement and cultural mindset that resonated beyond a singular trend, which would quickly spread it's prismatic wings into the heart of fashion, pop culture, and politics.

In addition to the explosion of experimental music and protest, a new generation of day-trippers and world travelers was born. Newly mellowed musicians, poets, and artists landed in India,

Japan, Africa, South America. There was a deep-rooted pursuit for new signifiers of counterculture—whether it was looking back into one's familial heritage or to artisans across the sea or around the world. There was a generative excitement about cultural exchanges that, in hindsight, can be worth a re-examination. Still, at the time, tie-dye filled this space of yearning.

With this in mind, an interesting story has emerged, which places tie-dye as it is known in its form today as an American invention. This misleading cultural mythology began with a brilliant ad campaign initiated by the household dye company Rit. On the brink of bankruptcy and at a moment in time when housewives of the fifties were giving way to a generation impacted by the Vietnam War, Rit was desperate to find a new audience. Up until this moment, Rit had been a beloved household staple used to dye many of the domestic necessities of the time. From bedspreads to drapes and clothing to rugs, Rit had established itself as the go-to for many homemakers across the country. Don Price, a risk-taking marketer, took on the challenge of reimagining Rit for the Summer of Love generation. Recognizing the rich and far-reaching histories of dye processes and uses from around the world, Price launched a marketing campaign to reinvent Rit as the must-have tool of psychedelic design, targeting the center of American counterculture: the artists of Greenwich Village. In New York City's most radical and left-leaning neighborhood, Price funded a homespun network of nonconformists and outsiders unable— and unwilling—to get desk jobs to experiment with Rit dyes as wearable art. In 1969, Price heard about the now-infamous Woodstock and funded artists to make hundreds of tie-dye t-shirts to sell at the festival. Was it masterminded, coincidence, or reverse engineered? Whatever it was, this early version of brand ambassadorship worked like gangbusters—in one summer, Rit leaped from pending bankruptcy to being of brand-name status and symbolic of a pivotal countercultural movement.

The seventies and eighties launched tie-dye into both high fashion and the mainstream, with Rit dye as the main ingredient. Retired window-decorator team Will and Eileen Richardson started a Rit-dyed fabric company in the West Village called Up-Tied. Their textiles were so impressive that fashion designer Halston immediately placed a five-thousand-dollar order—a substantial sum for this time.[1] Halston, once the milliner to Camelot—think Jackie O's pink pillbox hat—had a knack for forecasting fashion trends, and tie-dye was *it*. Couture designers followed and brought tie-dye to the runway. Celebrities like Liza Minelli, Ali MacGraw, and Anjelica Huston ushered tie-dye into the realm of glamour, splashed across *Look* magazine and the society pages. Rit dye, ubiquitous as a homespun product, transformed into a vehicle for high taste.

At this same moment, there was a proliferation of tie-dye as a kitchen sink activity. Children found unpredictable magic as they unfurled their dyed socks and underwear at summer camp, and teenagers proudly displayed their ragged dyed tees. Later, Generation X took tie-dye off the costume and, taking a cue from the "Boomer" generation, brought tie-dye back into mass circulation. Tie-dye became a signifier of alternative culture once again, particularly in the nineties with the rise of the Grunge movement. As a signifier, it could be both ironic and utopic, worn under lumberjack flannel shirts, hanging from the waists of skateboarders and the new generation of Dead Heads, all who equally relished in the prismatic colors of tie-dye. Those same qualities that tie-dye represented in the sixties and seventies—a desire to stay outside of the mainstream and build alternative kinds of community—were fostered in the nineties.

Today, we find tie-dye playing more of a new role representing the style and ethos of eco-chic, urban new age, and earth mama. It represents the aesthetics of sustainability and DIY culture. Tie-dye signifies something both wholesome and progressive. There has been a tremendous resurgence in the language around "hippie culture," although less about taking drugs and rock and roll, instead it engages conversations around climate change movements and global awareness. Tie-dye relates more to a larger desire to know how things work and how to make things happen, particularly in a digital world—people are glued to their computers and have fewer opportunities for real-life experiences. Tie-dye is an antidote to the desktop experience and instead provides hands-on experiences. The umbrella term of tie-dye has also been unpacked and released back into its deep origins of an ethnic art form. Shibori, Indigo, and Batik are terms and techniques that honor, ground, and educate. Today, tie-dye speaks to both high and low culture and expands outwards.

This book is an image-driven collage that locates tie-dye's re-emergence within countercultural and holistic movements, fashion, and art. In the U.S. post-Woodstock fashion has enabled tie-dye to transcend its often U.S.-centric cultural associations. Tie-dye's ancient origins, various and regional techniques, and myriad global cultural references are recognized and celebrated, from the couture catwalk to spirited street style, from summer camp cabins to the textile classroom. As told through images, this book makes visible why tie-dye has been a consistent presence and consistent reinvention in the 1960s through the present day. As we are finding ourselves working more and more within virtual spaces, tie-dye remains our social medium.

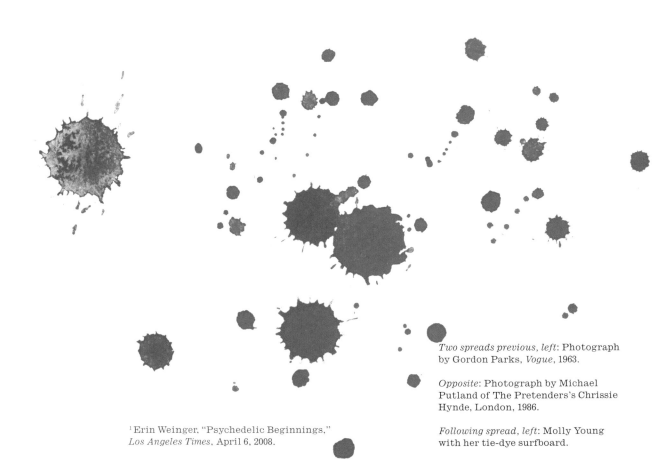

Two spreads previous, left: Photograph by Gordon Parks, *Vogue*, 1963.

Opposite: Photograph by Michael Putland of The Pretenders's Chrissie Hynde, London, 1986.

Following spread, left: Molly Young with her tie-dye surfboard.

[1] Erin Weinger, "Psychedelic Beginnings," *Los Angeles Times*, April 6, 2008.

The Resistance
Will Be Swirly

by Molly Young

"Don't expect perfection." That's the warning issued by Dona Z. Meilach, the author of a 1973 book called *Contemporary Batik and Tie-Dye: Methods, Inspiration, Dyes*. The admonition is about tie-dye specifically, but it could be about any technique that involves human intervention. The variations are infinite— and so, potentially, are the results.

Tie-dye is one of many "resist" techniques, which means exactly what it sounds like: a method in which bits of fabric are selectively prepared to repel color when dye is applied. In this case, the resistance involves ties, folds, binds, and knots, and they can be constructed from whatever is rattling around the maker's junk drawer. String, wire, raffia, beads, clips, Ping-Pong balls, and rubber bands are all fair game.

In America, it was The Countercultural Youth who first adopted tie-dye in the 1960s. Like scribbling on your jeans with a pen in chemistry class, it was an easy way to customize clothing. It was, by definition, a spontaneous and unpredictable process; in other words, hard to mess up. And it's a deeply practical method of ornamentation, too. Tie-dye hides stains like nothing else.

But The Countercultural Youth didn't invent it. The dead simplicity and pragmatism of tie-dye means it has been around for eons, though academics can't agree on where it started. Japan? China? Bali? West Africa? Mesoamerica? All of the above? Tie-dye appears on caves in India[1] and on tunics from the highlands of Peru.[2] Curiously enough, it seems to be a technique without fixed historical class associations. Those at the bottom of the ladder used tie-dye as a way to juice up raggedy old clothes, while those at the top pranced around in tie-dyed silks.[3] An exemplary "high-low" form, long before that term existed.

The version that bloomed in the 1960s carried nonspecific Eastern associations, suggesting that a wearer might be knowledgeable about topics such as Buddhism or yoga or esoteric psychedelic substances. It then quickly became shorthand for the DIY movement, anti-consumerism, and a general free-spiritedness and rejection of mass taste—a buffet of values broad enough that the motif's permeation into other subcultures seems, in retrospect, inevitable. It may have started with hippies, but tie-dye had a feminist art moment in the 1970s,[4] a skateboarding moment in the 1980s, a grunge moment in the 1990s, and a high-fashion moment in the 2000s before it ultimately exploded beyond all niche realms. Tie-dye is no longer synonymous with "handmade." It is now possible to buy a mass-produced tie-dye tube top for less than the cost of a cappuccino.[5]

As it happens, I grew up in a town that might hold the all-time record for highest tie-dye usage per capita. Bolinas, California, is an unincorporated coastal community that became a refuge for hippies, surfers, poets, astrologers and musicians in the 1960s. It was still heavily patchouli-scented during my 1990s childhood. I ate tofu sandwiches at the co-op and attended "creative movement experiences" at the community center. Tie-dye was so prevalent as to be invisible; pulling on my swirly rainbow pants was like drinking a glass of water or breathing air. An act of unquestioned neutrality.

None of the above, of course, answers the fundamental question about tie-dye, which is aesthetic. What *is it* about this imperfect, illegible, and stridently non-neutral design that could possibly attract such a wide swath of people over time and space? What is it about the shapes produced by tie-dyeing—irregular rosettes, donuts, spots, sunbursts, diamonds, stripes, chevrons— that appeal to a human visual sense that so often locates beauty in symmetry and order? Among the quirks of tie-dye production is that a true square shape cannot be produced; since woven fabrics stretch along the bias, imprinting a square parallel to a fabric's warp and weft is nearly impossible.[6] There is a metaphor at work here. Is it possible that tie-dye's periodical resurgences correlate with broader waves of social unease and uncertainty?

Having zero training in the world of data science, I love nothing more than to recklessly speculate on questions of precisely this nature. We live in a world of deep fakes and uncanny filters and proliferating bots; in under a decade we've witnessed the disappearance of consensus reality.[7] Tie-dye says: *The world is whirling down the drain along with your emotional equilibrium—why not wear a shirt that represents this state of emergency in quite literal terms, with hyperchaotic motifs and clashing hues?* It could represent a kind of homeopathy through style: cure like with like. Or, to go a bit darker, a strategy of "If you can't beat it, wear it." Either way, its particular form of beauty is not arbitrary. Fashion never is. If we're entering the abyss, we may as well dress for the occasion.

[1] Syliva Houghtelling, "The Emperor's Humbler Clothes: Textures of Courtly Dress in Seventeenth-Century South Asia," *Ars Orientalis*, Vol. 47 (2017).

[2] https://www.metmuseum.org/art/collection/search/314354.

[3] Shabd Simon-Alexander, *Tie-Dye: Dye It, Wear It, Share It* (New York: Clarkson Potter, 2013).

[4] https://www.marianclayden.com/textile-artworks.html— also the artists Phyllis Dukes and Karen Chang.

[5] https://us.shein.com/Tie-Dye-Bandana-Tube-Top-p-2221091-cat-2223.html.

[6] Laurie D. Webster, Kelley A. Hays-Gilpin, and Polly Schaafsma, "A New Look at Tie-Dye and the Dot-in-a-Square Motif in the Prehispanic Southwest," *Kiva*, Vol. 71, No. 3 (Spring, 2006).

[7] (And increasing generational anxiety.)

Gather

Immersed in the dye bath, gathered tightly, brilliant colors pool. Hues find tributaries as they seep deeper into the cloth. It is a vow that locks tightly as tie-dye is a transformative affair. It is one that mirrors the communal bond as there is magic in spreading so wide a varicolored fabric to revel in that pattern hidden within. It is a ticket to joy and this wonderment is of a convening spirit.

Photograph of Sari sisters wearing
NorBlack NorWhite.

Previous spread: Photograph by Florian
Joahn of Sharkkana and Zarina
Shukri in Fenty x ASAI Takeaway.

Opposite: Photograph by Elliot Landy
of Janis Joplin at the Woodstock
Festival, 1969.

Photography by My Wild Sparrows
of Georgie Lloyd in Nàdarra.

Opposite: Photograph of Maria
Lotta and Elena Saraeva by Natalya
Skvortsova for Sun Child.

Following spread: Photograph by
Henry Diltz of John Sebastian at the
Woodstock Festival, 1969.

Photograph by Byron Spencer for Pauly Bonomelli.

Opposite: Photograph by Max Miechowski for STORY mfg, London, 2019.

Previous spread, left: Photograph by Luna Khods of Mecha Clarke and Luis De Filippis in NorBlack NorWhite for 100% Silk.

Previous spread, right: Photograph by Sara Sani for Stüssy.

Photograph by Sajjad-Uddin
Muhammed of the artist duo
Aint Afraid.

The Dreamers

Tie-dye is the ornament of our dreams. From hot desert-scapes of sunset chevrons to galaxies far, far away, filled with psychedelic worm-holes, tie-dye has transportative powers. It is an endless summer day filled with sunshine in a field of buzzing daisies. Truly, it provides more than a colorful veneer to our wardrobe, it becomes the rolling gods-eye that allows us to see the world anew.

Photograph by Sara Sani.

Opposite: Photograph by Yoshi Uemura
for Land of Goshen by Raisa Yisrael.

Previous spread, left: Photograph by
Undine Markus of Kyle Lux.

Previous spread, right: Photograph
by Luna Khods of Mecha Clarke in
NorBlack NorWhite.

Two spreads previous, left: Directed by
Charlie Engman of Synphanie Mojica
for Collina Strada.

Photograph by Nicholas Reville for
Namu.

Opposite: Photograph by Hollie
Fernando for STORY mfg.

Photograph by Logan White
of Agnete Hegelund in Raquel Allegra.

Opposite: Photograph by Federico De
Angelis of Sanne de Roo in Alberta
Ferreti.

Following spread, *left*: Photograph
by Diane Sagnier of Pierre Podevyn in
Avellano.

Following spread, *right*: Photograph by
Pierre Podevyn of Diane Sagnier
in Avellano.

Photograph by Benjamin Provo of
his daughter, Zelda.

Opposite: Photograph by Isaac Park
of Jessie Park in Realisation, 2019.

Following spread, left: Photograph by
Hollie Fernando for in STORY mfg.

Following spread, right: Photograph by
Maiwenn Raoult of Kona Rose Jackson
in Soft Haus.

Two spreads following: Photograph by
Todd Supertramp of Nathan Watters
in Audrey Louise Reynolds.

Twist & Fold

Who could predict that after the labor of twisting, tying, and folding inherent to making tie-dye, it would drape so impeccably? With each stride, jump, and dip, tie-dye illuminates physicality and amplifies the motion of form. Patterns move rhythmically, swimmingly—making way for a mesmerizing flow.

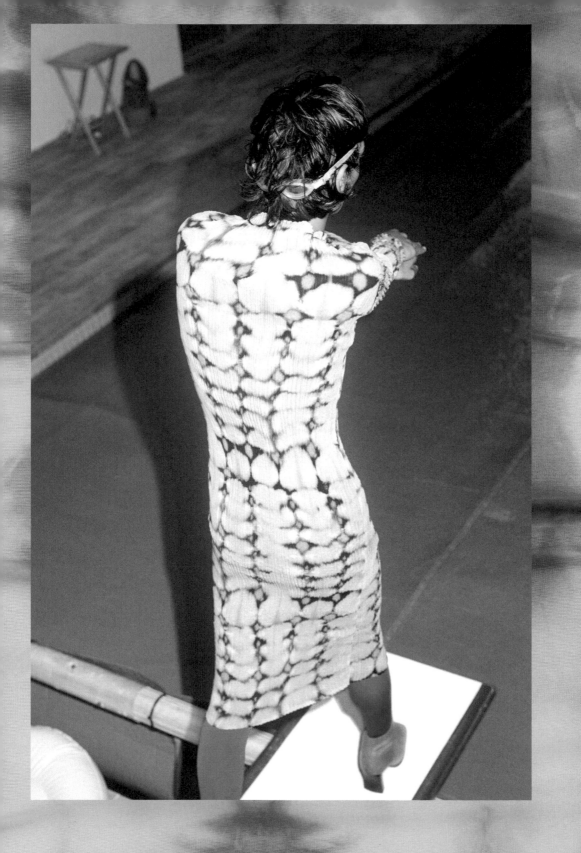

Film still from *Super Girls*, directed by Nicola Collie with director of photography Todd Blubaugh, clothes by Tory Sport.

Opposite: Photograph by Natalia Prada for Uniksea.

Previous spread, left: Photograph by Luna Khods of Samir in Julia Heuer.

Previous spread, right: Photograph by Rriley of Juliana Luna in abacaxi.

Two spreads previous, left: Photograph by Mathieu Fortin for Osei Duro.

Photograph by Michey Echeverry of
Germano Assuncao in Audrey Louise
Reynolds.

Opposite: Photograph by Melissa
Salaberry of Rodali Dutta in Coe
Textiles.

Previous spread, left: Photograph by
Tomra Palmer of Gravel & Gold in a
collaboration with Claire Lindsay-
McGinn.

Photograph by Andrés Altamirano
of Pau Bertolini in Audrey Louise
Reynolds.

Opposite: Photograph by Alice Carron
of Hayley McKinlay in a Maison Sara
Dakhli blouse and a Woola La skirt,
styling by Julie Simoneau and hair
and makeup by Elodie Lacambra.

Photograph by Luna Khods of Linh in
Julia Heuer.

Opposite: Photograph by Ira Chernova
of Nyadhuor Deng in KkCo.

Saturated Street Style

From the fleeting fuchsia and vermilion streaks of speeding race cars to the gridded geometry of a Shibuya crosswalk, dazzling city lights and dull concrete are the perfect backdrops to make the fantastic colors of fashion truly pop. Tie-dye's bold brights never tip-toe—they tango with the concrete jungle. They dazzle and purr, creating a wondrous composition, a perfection that need not be tamed.

Photograph for KkCo.

Opposite: Photograph by Szymon Brzóska of Courtney Trop, Jo Rosenthal, Reese Blutstein, and Molly Blutstein.

Previous spread, *left*: Photograph by Shoichi Aoki.

Following spread, *left*: Photograph by Cheyenne El-Khoury of Grece Ghanem.

Following spread, *right*: Photograph by Erin Oldenburg of Jeffrey Wilkins in By My Grace.

Photograph of Leandra Medine of Man Repeller.

Opposite: Photograph by Romina Introini of Tamu McPherson.

Previous spread, left: Photograph by Natalya Skvortsova of Anna Vititina for Sun Child.

Previous spread, right: Photograph of Frances Aaternir in DANNIJO.

Self-portrait by Julia Prislin.

Opposite: Photograph by Annelise Howard Phillips of Ibada Wadud in Triple Cream NYC by Charlotte Greville; styled by Lorri Sendel.

Photograph by Kevin Gonzalez of Aleali May in ASAI Takeaway.

Opposite: Photograph by Ema Hewitt of Achol Manoah in HEW.

Following spread, left: Photograph by Vitalina.

Following spread, right: Photograph by Lea Winkler of Arielle Chambers with Andrea Bergart bag.

Photograph of Ami Amiaya and
Aya Amiaya during Milan Fashion
Week in Milan, Italy, 2020.

Ecstatic Visions

As our minutes so often die in the digital void, tie-dye brings us back to something sacred. Preparing a bath, gathering cloth, planning a design: these are the things of ritual. We are brought to a sensual moment making tie-dye. We touch the bound cloth, we dip with our hands fully and we are slowed to a new rhythm. It is a moment that cracks open our quotidian, if only to let in more mystical powers.

Photograph by Tsao Daniel of Jundan
Chen in Imane Ayissi.

Previous spread, *left*: Photograph by
Undine Markus for KkCo.

Photograph by Helena Christensen
of Clara McGregor in Audrey Lousie
Reynolds.

Opposite: Photograph by Michal Smith
of Stella Thepaut in Manifest Color.

Photograph by Yoshi Uemura for Land
of Goshen by Raisa Yisrael.

Photograph by Henry Clarke of Maria
Schiano, *Vogue*, 1968.

Following spread, left: Photograph by
Talaya Centeno, *WWD*, 2002.

Following spread, right: Photograph by
Akshay Sharma for NorBlack NorWhite.

Two spreads following: Photograph
by Harrie Verstappen of artist
Yayoi Kusama, 1971.

Self-portrait by Mae Lutz.

Following spread, *left*: Self-portrait by Willy Somma for Upstate.

Following spread, *right*: Photograph for KkCo.

Two spreads following: Photograph by Margo Ducharme of Kat Hessen for Raquel Allegra.

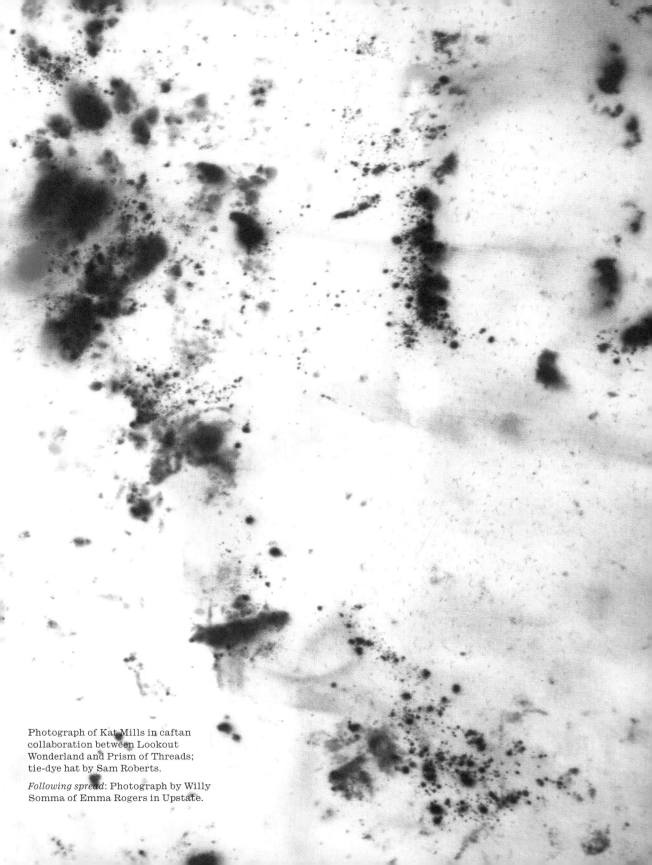

Photograph of Kat Mills in caftan
collaboration between Lookout
Wonderland and Prism of Threads;
tie-dye hat by Sam Roberts.

Following spread: Photograph by Willy
Somma of Emma Rogers in Upstate.

Prisms & Color

From Flower Power to the catwalks of haute couture,
tie-dye radiates a radical rainbow. *Le freak, c'est chic!*
Patterns and colors boogie and comingle, merging into
kaleidoscopic ecstasy. The psychedelic aesthetic, an
escalator trip to the cosmos, transcend rationality,
making each spurt of color another wildly untethered
moment.

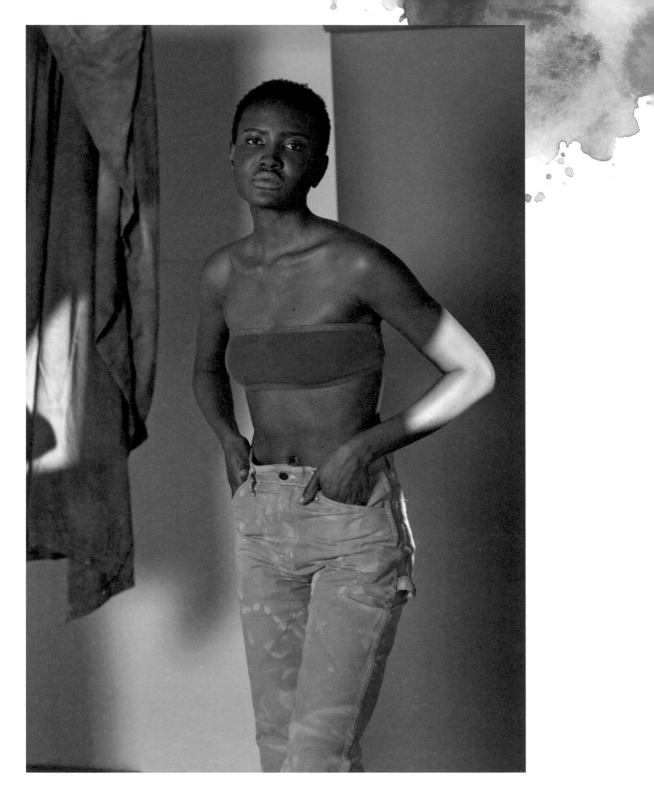

Photograph by King Foxx for Tiedyefel.

Opposite: Photograph by Willy Somma
of Munira Zulfadli in a VPL top and
Upstate × Willy Somma pants.

Previous spread, left: Photograph
by Mara Hoffman of Lizzy Yusuff in
Mara Hoffman.

Photograph of Molly Young surfing in
Mexico.

Opposite: Photograph of Danielle
and Jodie, DANNIJO founders and
designers, in their designs with Jodie's
daughter Margaux.

Following spread: Photograph by
Joseph Maddon.

Photograph by Jessica Steddom of
Mary Lawless Lee.

Opposite: Photograph by Mark Sennet
of actress Drew Barrymore, 1990.

Following spread, left: Photograph
by Curt Saunders of Ladin Awad in
abacaxi.

Following spread, right: Photograph
by Kyle Warfield of Henry Boamah
in Extra Vitamins dyed by Julia
Belamarich.

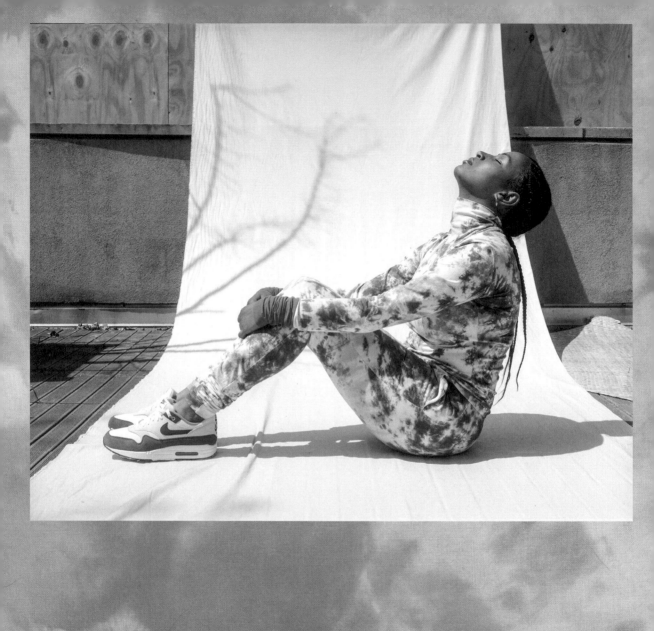

Photograph by Enoch Adeleye for
Yina's Kulture, creative direction by
Stephanie James.

Opposite: Photograph by Luna Khods
of Samir in Julia Heuer.

Following spread, left: Self-portrait by
Blanca Miro Scrimieri.

Following spread, right: Photograph by
Bryce Thompson for Banana Moon.

Opposite: Photograph by Akshay Sharma for NorBlack NorWhite.

Previous spread: Photograph of Trev skateboarding in Flomotion.

Aurora Borealis

In nature, bold colors with high-contrast patterns, like tie-dye, both serve as protective camouflage and signal drama. Perhaps, too, tie-dye is like the aurora borealis, commanding attention with its tranquil display of color that washes the polar skies. It's a glorious bath that belies the underlying drama of the Sun's particles colliding with the Earth's gases. The wonders of the natural world compliment and inform the mysterious ways in which tie-dye represents our inner selves.

Photograph by Willy Somma of Emma
Rogers and Laura Tucker for Upstate.

Previous spread, *left*: Photograph
by Solenne Choi of Macy Gupta in
Nàdarra.

Following spread, *left*: Photograph by
Federico De Angelis of Sanne de Roo
in Alberta Ferretti.

Following spread, *right*:Photograph by
Mark Cobrasnake of Ava Cutrone in
Mimi Prober.

Two spreads following: Photograph by
Shawn Hanna for Raquel Allegra.

Opposite: Photograph by Hansraj Dochaniya of Shia Rai in NorBlack NorWhite.

Previous spread: Photograph by Willy Somma of Emma Rogers in Rachel Comey.

Two spreads previous, left: Photograph by Akshay Sharma for NorBlack NorWhite.

Two spreads previous, right: Photograph by Marguerite for abacaxi.

Three spreads previous, left: Photograph by Rebecca Höltgen of Annika-Marie Leik for Suzusan with styling and art direction by Akiko Stiebeling.

Three spreads previous, right: Photograph by Natalya Skvortsova of Elena Saraeva in Sun Child.

Photograph by Nick DeLieto of Irene Stepanenko in Mimi Prober.

Opposite: Photograph by Nick DeLieto of Irene Stepanenko in Mimi Prober.

Following spread, left: Self-portrait by Curie Lee in her own design.

Two spreads following: Photograph by Keith Oshiro for Raquel Allegra.

Acknowledgments

I have to start by thanking my parents, Monica and Kevin McNamara, for inspiring this publication and bringing the beauty and complexity of counterculture and tie-dye into my life at an early age. Thanks to my husband Jim Drain and daughter Frida Lu for their thoughtful input, generous patience, and ever-inspiring tie-dye wardrobes.

Sincere gratitude to my tireless editor, Julie Schumacher, who went out of her way to make this book come to life—thank you for your perseverance, creativity, and support! This book is here because of you. I also want to thank my designer, Hilary duPont, whose joyful problem-solving and enthusiasm were unwavering and unflappable. A special thanks to Supriya Malik who choreographed the final push to get this book off the ground, and Kiernan Pazdar and Kara Cox whose research and organization were indispensable.

A special thank you to Cole Hill at Condé Nast for all his help; and to @natasha_sneba, Alice Carron, Nicola Collie, and Mimi Prober.

And lastly, I want to extend my gratitude to all the incredible photographers, artists, designers, and creatives I encountered while researching and making this book. Thank you for sharing your extraordinary work, your stories, archives, and rich histories, each of which has impacted this project.